Minnesota
TIMBERWOLVES

BY K.C. KELLEY

Published by The Child's World®
1980 Lookout Drive • Mankato, MN 56003-1705
800-599-READ • www.childsworld.com

Cover: © AP Images/Ben Margot.
Interior Photographs ©: AP Images: Ann Heisenfelt 9; Andy Clayton-King
10; Jim Moore 26. Dreamstime.com: Kent Wolter 12; Danny Raustadt 13.
Imagn/USA Today Sports: Russ Isabella 5, 26; Harrison Burden 26. News-
com: Jeff Wheeler/TNS 6, 25; Icon SMI 17; Jeff Wheeler/MCT 18; John
Doman/KRT 21; Marlin Levison/MCT 22; Carlos Gonzalez/MCT 29.

ISBN 9781503824713
LCCN 2018964346

Printed in the United States of America
PA02416

ABOUT THE AUTHOR

K.C. Kelley is a huge sports fan who has
written more than 150 books for kids.
He has written about football, basketball,
soccer, and even auto racing! He lives in
Santa Barbara, California.

TABLE OF

CONTENTS

GO, TIMBERWOLVES!

Are the Timberwolves coming out of the Minnesota woods? The team struggled for most of the 2000s. In 2018, Minnesota made the playoffs for the first time since 2004. Led by star **center** Karl-Anthony Towns, the 'Wolves might be ready to roar! Let's meet the Timberwolves.

Up, up, and away! Big Karl-Anthony Towns leads the Timberwolves with great shooting skills like this.

5

Andrew Wiggins nails a jumper. His shooting touch has helped the Timberwolves win.

WHO ARE THE TIMBERWOLVES?

The Minnesota Timberwolves are one of 30 NBA teams. The Timberwolves play in the Northwest Division of the Western Conference. The other Northwest Division teams are the Denver Nuggets, the Oklahoma City Thunder, the Portland Trail Blazers, and the Utah Jazz. The Timberwolves have tough battles with their Northwest Division **rivals**!

WHERE THEY CAME FROM

The NBA added an **expansion team** in 1989. The Timberwolves were the first NBA team in Minnesota since the Lakers left for Los Angeles in 1960. Fans sent in ideas for the new team's name. Then Minnesota cities voted on the most popular ideas. Timberwolves won! Minnesota is home to more timberwolves than any other state.

Star forward Christian Laettner started his long NBA career with Minnesota.

Time to celebrate! Robert Covington leads the cheers after another Minnesota win.

WHO THEY PLAY

The Timberwolves play 82 games each season. They play 41 games at home and 41 on the road. The Timberwolves play four games against each of the other Northwest Division teams. They play 36 games against other Western Conference teams. The Timberwolves also play each of the teams in the Eastern Conference twice. That's a lot of basketball! Each June, the winners of the Western and Eastern Conferences play each other in the NBA Finals.

WHERE THEY PLAY

The Timberwolves have played at the Target Center since 1990. The arena is located in Minneapolis. It has a green roof. That is, the roof is covered with grass and plants. The Target Center is also home to the Minnesota Lynx (right). That team plays in the **WNBA**. The Lynx are four-time WNBA champs!

13

TARGET○CENTER

The Minneapolis Dogs? The dog is not for the team. It is a symbol of the Target stores.

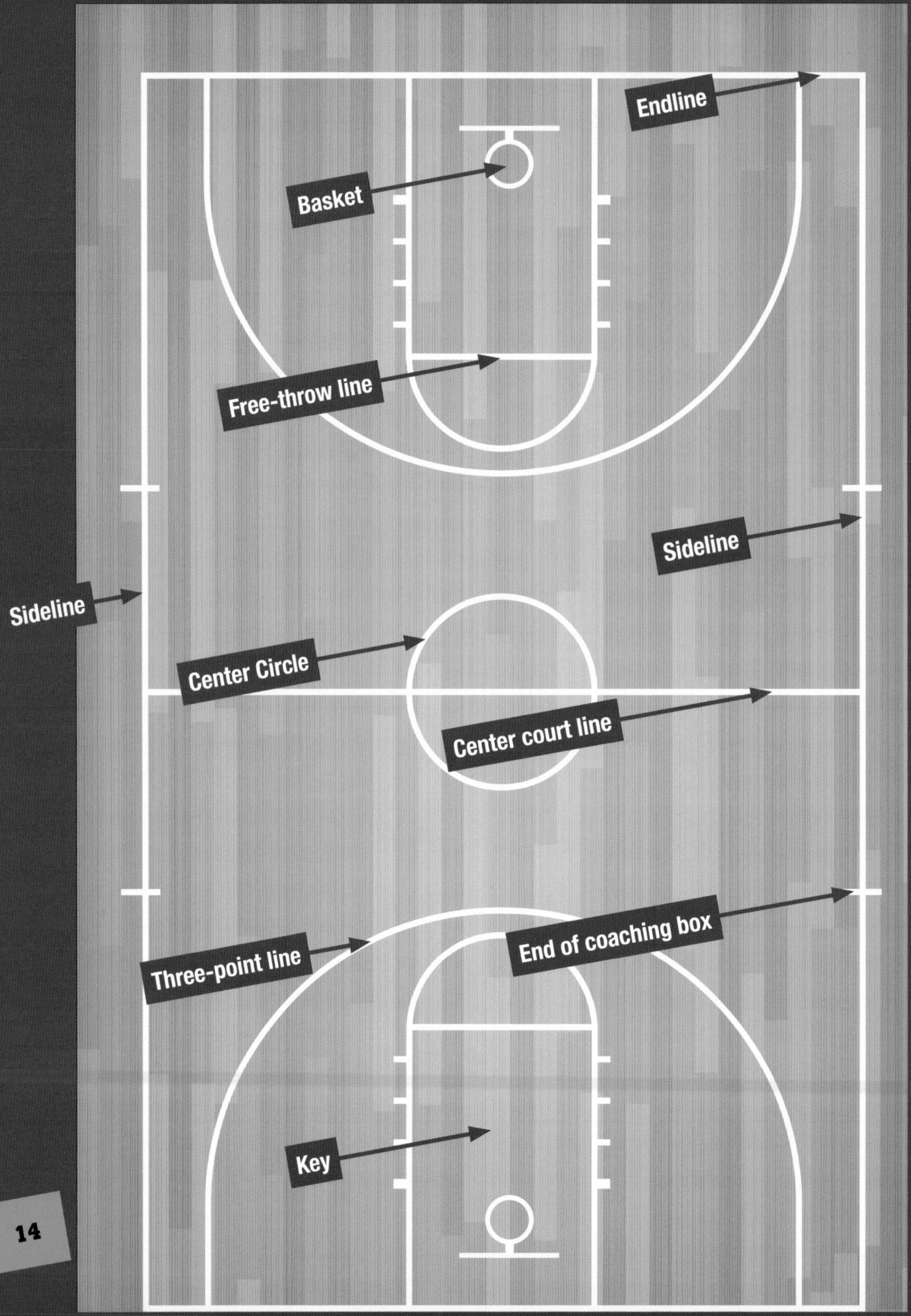

Endline

Basket

Free-throw line

Sideline

Sideline

Center Circle

Center court line

Three-point line

End of coaching box

Key

THE BASKETBALL COURT

An NBA court is 94 feet long and 50 feet wide (28.6 m by 15.24 m). Nearly all the courts are made from hard maple wood. Rubber mats under the wood help make the floor springy. Each team paints the court with its logo and colors. Lines on the court show the players where to take shots. The diagram on the left shows the important parts of the NBA court.

The Target Center is a busy place! With concerts, meetings, and sports events, more than 1 million people go there each year.

GOOD TIMES

The Timberwolves' best season came in 2003–04. They won a team-record 58 games. They also won the Northwest Division for the first time. In the Western Conference finals, they lost to the Los Angeles Lakers. In 2016, Minnesota poured in 144 points in a win over the New Orleans Pelicans. That was a Timberwolves' team record for points.

During the 2004 Western Conference finals, Minnesota's Wally Szczerbiak drove to the hoop.

Indiana blocked this Timberwolves shot in 2010. Minnesota was used to it. The team lost 67 games that year!

TOUGH TIMES

The Timberwolves got off to a slow start in the NBA. They lost 60 games in their first season. They didn't have a winning record until their ninth season. Minnesota's 2009–10 season was pretty bad, too. The Timbewolves lost a team-record 67 games. They are bouncing back, though, and made the playoffs in 2018.

ALL THE RIGHT MOVES

Kevin Garnett was a star for Minnesota for 12 seasons. He played center, a position for tall players. Garnett used his long arms to grab **rebounds**. On offense, he was very quick. Though he was almost seven feet tall, he could dribble around smaller players. Garnett was an all-around star!

Players can get rebounds after any missed shot. On offense, they can then shoot again. On defense, they start moving toward the opposite basket with the ball.

Kevin Garnett spent the first 14 seasons of his great career with the Timberwolves. He started when he was only 19!

21

Before moving to the Cavaliers, Kevin Love played fiercely for the Timberwolves.

HEROES THEN

Kevin Garnett moved right from high school to the Timberwolves in 1995. From the start, he was a superstar. He is Minnesota's best player ever. Garnett scored more points and had more rebounds than any other Timberwolves player. He will certainly be named to the Basketball Hall of Fame. Kevin Love led the NBA in rebounding in 2011. Now he's a star with the Cleveland Cavaliers.

Today's top star in Minnesota is center Karl Anthony-Towns. Tall and strong, he is the team's top scorer. He also pulls down lots of rebounds. **Forward** Andrew Wiggins can also score a lot of points. **Veteran** forward Robert Covington joined the team in 2018. His scoring skills will help Towns and Wiggins.

Karl-Anthony Towns shows off the dunking form that has helped make him one of the top young players in the league.

WHAT THEY WEAR

NBA players wear a **tank top** jersey. Players wear team shorts. Each player can choose his own sneakers. Some players also wear knee pads or wrist guards.

Each NBA team has more than one jersey style. The pictures at left show some of the Timberwolves' jerseys.

The NBA basketball (left) is 29.5 inches around. It is covered with leather. The leather has small bumps called pebbles.

The pebbles on a basketball help players grip it.

TEAM STATS

Here are some of the all-time career records for the Minnesota Timberwolves. These stats are complete through all of the 2018–19 NBA regular season.

GAMES

Kevin Garnett	970
Sam Mitchell	757

POINTS PER GAME

Karl-Anthony Towns	22.3
Tony Campbell	20.6

THREE-POINTERS

Anthony Peeler	465
Kevin Love	440

REBOUNDS PER GAME

Kevin Love	12.2
Karl Anthony-Towns	11.9

STEALS PER GAME

Ricky Rubio	2.1
Tyrone Corbin	2.0

FREE-THROW PCT.

Terrell Brandon	.895
Kevin Martin	.886

RICKY RUBIO

ASSISTS PER GAME

Ricky Rubio	8.5
Stephon Marbury	8.3

GLOSSARY

center *(SEN-ter)* a basketball position that plays near the basket

expansion team *(ex-PAN-shun TEEM)* in sports, a team that is added to an existing league

forward *(FORE-word)* a player in basketball who usually plays away from the basket

mascot *(MASS-kot)* a costumed character who helps fans cheer

rebounds *(REE-boundz)* missed shots that bounce to players on the court

rivals *(RYE-vuhlz)* two people or groups competing for the same thing

tank top *(TANK TOP)* a style of shirt that has straps over the shoulders and no sleeves

veteran *(VETT-er-un)* a player with several years of experience in a sport

WNBA Women's National Basketball Association

FIND OUT MORE

IN THE LIBRARY

Schaller, Bob and Dave Harnish. *The Everything Kids' Basketball Book (3rd Edition).* New York, NY: Adams Media, 2017.

Sports Illustrated Kids (editors). Big Book of Who: Basketball. New York, NY: Sports Illustrated Kids, 2015.

Whiting, Jim. *The NBA: A History of Hoops: Minnesota Timberwolves.* Mankato, MN: Creative Paperbacks, 2017.

ON THE WEB

Visit our website for links about the Minnesota Timberwolves:
childsworld.com/links

Note to Parents, Teachers, and Librarians: We routinely verify our Web links to make sure they are safe and active sites. So encourage your readers to check them out!

INDEX